ALL GAS, NO BRAKES

What it Takes to Go From Bankrupt to Millionaire

BY

NATE KENNEDY

ALL GAS, NO BRAKES

Copyright © 2021 by Nate Kennedy

All rights reserved. No part of this publication may be reproduced, distributed, or transmitted in any form or by any means, including photocopying, recording, or other electronic or mechanical methods, without the prior written permission of the author, except in the case of brief quotations embodied in critical reviews and certain other non-commercial uses permitted by copyright law.

Ordering Information: Quantity sales. Special discounts are available on quantity purchases by corporations, associations, and others. Orders by U.S. trade bookstores and wholesalers.

DREAMSTARTERS

www.DreamStartersPublishing.com

NATE KENNEDY

Table of Contents

Introduction 4

All Gas, No Brakes 8

Focus Less on Loss and More on Solutions 18

Do Less 31

Empower Your Team 40

Don't Seek Counsel from False Prophets 48

Decisions, Decisions 59

Don't Stop Marketing 75

Know the Rules of Engagement 87

Mind Your Own Business 93

Keep Your Inner Circle Small 100

The Non-Negotiables 112

Conclusion 119

Introduction

Everything has a reason, and it is often the reason that matters. It is overlooked, at least for a better part of our lives. A lot of us dwell in the past, thinking how we could've avoided a certain situation, or how things could've "turned out different." To me, that is just absurd. Change is constant, and it is bound to happen whether we like it or not. We can prepare ourselves beforehand or just go with it. There is no other option on the table.

Entrepreneurs that have stepped up to achieve their goals and targets have been often bombarded with situations that do not turn out the way they want them to be. People tend to fall into this victim mindset, thinking that they are not worthy or something wasn't meant to be. It's disappointing. No one knows what tomorrow holds. That does not mean you give up chasing your dreams or give in to the hardships of the time and call it quits. That is not the way of an entrepreneur, and that is certainly not the way I operate. What most of us are missing is a simple element of resiliency.

Resiliency is nothing more than the ability to stay committed to a goal, a thought, or a way of life, despite all the odds stacked up against someone. Take it from someone who is a proud and resilient survivor of the massive economic crash that happened in the not-too-distant past. While many people I knew were contemplating suicide, I was moving forward. I found myself to be someone who continued to instill a sense of hope, confidence, and resilience. Like everyone, I've been on the receiving end of harsher times. It has not always been a "living my dream" kind of life. What ultimately mattered was how I was able to remain 'resilient' and press charge. It was this skill, capability, and strength that helped me stare into the face of challenges and come out victorious.

I have learned throughout my journey that many great entrepreneurs have gone through such hardships. **What separated them apart from the ones who couldn't make it big was their resilience**. On top of that is great mentors. They help entrepreneurs like you and me forge paths ahead to find the kind of success we've been yearning for all this time.

This book is my attempt to reach out to the masses, especially those who have just started their journey as an entrepreneur. Throughout this book, I intend to share what I've been through, what I've learned, and what I've picked up to take away the guessing game and put entrepreneurs in the driving seat. Even as an entrepreneur, having someone guide you through the different phases of your journey goes a long way. You learn where to focus on, what to work on, and how to ignore everything else that is a waste of time.

ALL GAS, NO BRAKES

The idea of becoming an entrepreneur is quite exciting. Let me first clarify something: If you are trying to become an entrepreneur because you are drawn to the flashy cars and luxurious lifestyle, and so on, then that is not the start. It is a full-time, lifelong struggle that requires utmost commitment, perseverance, and dedication. At the center of this entire journey will be your resiliency.

There are thousands of books out there, but most of them only go on to talk about general aspects of being an entrepreneur. They never share practical lessons you can implement into your life. That is where I decided to step in.

For those who do not know me, I am an entrepreneur and I fall into the marketing side of the business. Marketing has been my go-to field, and rightfully so. My journey has been nothing short of a roller-coaster ride, especially since I went right through the global recession that hit the world (and hit it hard). I went bankrupt, but the next year I emerged from the ashes and made my way back to the top. My stories will teach entrepreneurs how to avoid misleading "get rich overnight" ideas and pursue their dreams in a more practical way.

It does not matter whether you work in real estate, services, or any other sector. These lessons are applicable across the board. You do not need any specialized knowledge to get things going your way. You just need a bit of guidance, inspiration, and ideas to begin your journey the right way. With that being said, it's time to dive into the world of resiliency and learn how to propel yourself from rock bottom all the way to living your ideal lifestyle. **It all begins when you step on the gas.**

Chapter 1

All Gas, No Brakes

Have you ever had that "lightbulb" moment? Something you thought would be the next big thing, or just a great idea for something personal? We've all had at least one moment like this. The question is: Do you pursue that idea, or let it go?

For many, the lightbulb moments are passed up. You decide it was not worth pursuing or feel too distracted by life. Who knows what you could have done with that idea. Or how far you could have gone with it. Instead, you enjoy the idea for a bit and then hit the brakes. Life returns back to normal. This happens every day in small and large decisions.

My lightbulb moment was back in 2018 and I should have gone full gas towards it. Instead, I hit the brakes. I waited a few years before picking it back up. It's because of this experience that I believe we should go full gas towards our goals and keep our feet off the brakes. Amelia Earhart once said, "The most effective way to do it, is to do it." Simple and yet completely true. Reaching your goals is about moving towards them and never stopping until you reach the finish line.

In 2018, I wanted to switch from Marketing Agency to a Media Company. I had done work like this in 2006 with my friend Mark Evans DM, but that was at a much smaller scale. My business had evolved into a full-service Marketing Agency and I was ready to make a Pivot. I reached out to Mark to talk about getting my idea off the ground. I visited him in Florida and talked with a couple of other guys. I was ready to take this idea and run with it. But the moment I got home, I started overcomplicating it. Between that and life, the idea got buried. I chose to hit the brakes and kept chugging along.

Fast forward to January 2020, and I decided it was time to unbury that idea. I wanted to give it more than just a thought. I told my wife that I wanted to wake up in the morning, send an email, and then be done with my workday. That was the dream for me. I started investing on the idea in May and launched a new media company right in the middle of the coronavirus pandemic. It's been one year since we started and have already grown the business massively. In the first year, we drove over $1.5MM in revenue by simply sending emails we collected with our 1-Step Funnel. There has been nothing but massive room for growth.

If I had followed this idea in 2018, who knows where the business would be now. I might have made millions in revenue and grown far more than originally imagined. But I didn't start in 2018 and I missed out on those opportunities.

However, waiting until 2020 put me in the right mindset to go all in. I put everything into it. I removed my safety net and parted ways with all my high-paying clients. I put all of my focus into building this business. I had no choice but to sink or swim and, with everything on the line, I had all the incentive to keep pushing. I kept moving forward until I got to where I am now. I could kick myself for not starting back in 2018, but am thankful I went full gas and did this now.

Why Do We Hit the Brakes?

Rudyard Kipling, the author of *The Jungle Book*, famously said: *"If you don't get what you want, it's a sign either that you did not seriously want it, or that you tried to bargain over the price."* We hit the brake for two reasons: either because we didn't want to put in the effort, or we were worried about the cost of our lives. I want to add another idea to this; we often hit the brakes because we lose direction.

NATE KENNEDY

Starting from the top, we often hit the brakes because we don't want to put serious effort into our goals. If you don't put the effort in, it's because you may not want it. It's easy to have ideas, but it's much harder to work on those ideas. Turning an idea into something tangible is hard work, and often worthwhile. People share great ideas all the time, but want you to do the work for them. So it often stops at an idea. This is why I ask people to do the work on their ideas before I invest any of my time. I often never hear back from them. It's hard work to turn an idea into a profitable business and if I hear back from them, I invest more time to get them get rolling. Remember - having an idea is great, but everyone has one. Keeping an idea alive is about putting in the work to succeed.

Distractions are another idea killer. People get easily distracted by other things in life. It happens all too frequently. Even I've fallen into the trap. We get a great idea and as we begin to dig deeper, we realize the risk involved. Our instinct is to stay inside our comfort bubble instead of addressing the risk. It makes it easy to get distracted and return to your 9-5 job. It's what you know. Distractions are everywhere, from family troubles to social pressure, and even blowing a tire on the highway. These are put in your way to help you remain average, but you can plow right over them and determine your own success. When you get distracted, just remember that someone else is working to turn a similar idea into a million-dollar business. Life can get in the way of turning ideas into reality, so you have to find the time. For me, this meant firing all my high-paying clients and putting everything into my idea. Without a safety net, I couldn't turn back and continue doing what was considerably less risky.

Kipling said if we don't go towards our goals, it is because we are worried about the cost or the price we'll pay. I always think of this as the risk associated with trying something new. Maybe we're afraid of making a mistake or failing at a new venture. Maybe we're worried that we'll lose everything and be left at square one. These are all valid fears, but they can't set you back. Many people will dip a foot into an idea or project while having the other securely on the shore and ready to pull you back at the slightest sign of a challenge. The fact is, challenges are going to come up. You are going to make mistakes. From those mistakes, you learn and develop your ideas. By only putting in half the effort, you're guaranteed to fail because you won't gain the momentum you need to move forward and develop your idea into a reality. You need to fully immerse yourself into getting an idea off the ground, so that even when mistakes are made, you won't fail. You put everything towards your goals.

Lastly, I think that people hit the brakes because they lose direction or don't have an end goal in mind. This happened in 2018 when I overcomplicated my idea, but it can and does happen to everyone. You can easily lose your direction if you don't have a clear-cut destination in mind. It often happens when you focus on all the choices instead of just making a choice. One of the things I see entrepreneurs trying to find is the "perfect" idea or the "perfect" option, but while they're looking, they're letting go of perfectly good opportunities and never getting started. They're looking for the ultimate money maker and, in that search, end up passing by great opportunities. They often end up never actually picking a direction to start. Another way of overcomplicating the process is trying to start everything at once. This is easy to see when people try to market across all social media platforms at once. They don't take the time to focus on just one area and develop that. In both cases, the direction was lost. Instead, we're left wandering around and hoping for the best. My recommendation is to focus on your idea. Have success in one thing before trying to have success at everything. You make a choice and go for it.

All Gas

Going full throttle towards your goals is the only way to truly succeed at them. I can't express how much "putting my all" into goals has helped me and I'm so thankful it has worked. Hitting the brakes on my original idea was a learning experience and I encourage everyone to give it their all. When you have an idea, go for it and don't wait for the perfect time or opportunity. With my current team, I emphasize the word "executing" or getting things moving. It's better to try and get it wrong, than to not try at all. I'd rather see them execute something and get it wrong than just sit on their hands and do nothing. Move towards your goals and use all gas, no brakes.

The idea is to build up momentum. Once you start something, go with it. There will be hiccups along the way and you can't avoid making mistakes. Instead of worrying about them or dwelling on how things went wrong, learn from them and move on. The only person who ends up suffering is **you.** If you choose to waste your time thinking of the past, you'll end up missing out on the opportunities to build a better future.

Mistakes are a major part of our lives. Before any tangible success, there has to be a mistake. Entrepreneurs and business-minded people around the world have invested a significant part of their lives trying to learn from mistakes. They have not only managed to learn from their mistakes, but take corrective actions accordingly. Remember: **the day you think you know it all is the day you will stop learning completely.** Failures are the golden opportunities to learn from. It may not feel all that nice, but it is essential. Instead of running away from failure, prepare for it. Instead of reacting negatively to a situation that did not turn out the way you anticipated, be more receiving. Learn through feedback and research on how things went wrong, then apply that. Do not dwell because your momentum is on the line.

Consistency is key, and momentum is only maintained if you are consistent. The end goal may seem miles away but that does not mean you should stop. It only takes one step to move a step closer. By being consistent and resilient, you will make it all the way through.

Brakes (used at the wrong time) will kill your business. More importantly, they will kill your dreams. A major failure can make you a little gun-shy for a long period. If you notice this is happening, you are focusing on the wrong things in life. You are focusing on where you have been rather than where you want to go --- a recipe that will never make a millionaire.

ALL GAS, NO BRAKES

HIT THE GAS

What are some lightbulb moments that you've had? Think hard!

_____
_____
_____
_____
_____
_____
_____

Why didn't you pursue them? Be honest with yourself!

_____
_____
_____
_____
_____
_____
_____

NATE KENNEDY

"Whatever you do, work at it with all your heart, as working for the lord."

Col 3:23

Chapter 2

Focus Less on Loss and More on Solutions

Growing up, I spent a lot of time trying to build a business. As a 10-year-old, that's not very easy. But I worked hard to shovel snow or cut grass, just trying to make a buck. I even created a pretty lucrative video business that failed when my mom found out. I think I always had that drive to build my own business. My first official business was started in 2005 when I created Laurus Funding Group, a mortgage company.

It was my first lucrative business as an adult and I was excited to create it. Of course, no man is an island, so I brought in a lot of great people to help me out. It worked so well and I thought that the success was because I was just great at what I did. In all honesty, it was just the times. The industry was booming and anyone could have made money. They just had to have the kahunas put together a business plan and go for it. They had to take a step forward and make it happen.

  I took that step. In two years, I grew that company from a mortgage company to one that was also a real estate company, construction company, and investment company. We built high-end homes, financed others, sold properties, and did all sorts of stuff all in a short two-year period. It was wildly successful and I was ecstatic. We built a multimillion-dollar portfolio with great cash flow coming in. I felt 100% secure in the success of my business.

  I was getting excited for 2008 and then the housing bubble burst. I was suddenly a part of the Great Recession. It was financially devastating to me, my company, and many of my friends and colleagues. I lost everything and all of a sudden. There was zero cash flow. I went from living large and paying for everything to having no money come in. It was all gone. I met with an attorney and had to make some tough decisions, eventually declaring corporate bankruptcy. I sat there feeling like a massive failure.

Losing everything was hard. It wasn't just my company that was gone, but also my home, my income, my pride and so many things of value. I was lucky enough to have my wife (girlfriend at the time) and another friend stand strong in my corner. Others disappeared. Between the bankruptcy, foreclosure on my properties, and other massive losses, I slipped into serious depression.

In a 2019 Forbes and Krueger study, it was determined that people who faced any sort of job, financial, or housing-related crisis during the recession had a greater chance of clinical depression, anxiety, panic attacks, and overall worse mental health. I wasn't alone in my feelings of depression. Looking back on that time, I just remember being massively depressed.

I had been trying to find a change in my foreclosed home so that I would have some cash. Life changed drastically and it was rough. But I've always been solution-oriented. After dwelling on my failure, I started looking for solutions to my problems. I realized that searching for change wasn't going to work. Staying in a mindset of being a "failure" or depressed wasn't going to work for me. It wasn't going to fix anything. I realized that if I'm not doing anything, then nothing was going to change. If I continued to sit there, I was going to be even more broke by the next week, and possibly even more depressed.

I had to flip a switch and ask myself what I was going to do. Was I going to sit there and let things get worse, or was I going to do something about it? Once I decided to do something, I had to analyze my steps. What was I going to do first? What could I do today to be in a more positive situation tomorrow?

While this sounds easy in theory, it's much harder in practice. The point is that I wanted to try.

Failure is a Learning Moment

A business is not a venture without risk, and no matter how perfect your plan is, there is always going to be a point when you lose. It can be as simple as losing a client, or as large as losing the whole business. We can't always win. This is important. We cannot win 100% of the time, that's not realistic. They happen in business, our everyday situations, and life in general. When someone tells you that they always win or don't lose, then that's just more wishful thinking than anything else.

Losses happen. The most important thing about them is what we learn from those losses. Step one is to not dwell on our losses. If we spend our time sinking into failure and really focusing on it, then it becomes our whole world. Failure takes over everything we've ever wanted and flips the mindset. We go from being driven to succeed to becoming bitter about our obstacles. It only takes one loss to destroy the drive and stagnate.

My son is really into sports right now and driven to win in every game. His level of competition and drive pushes him to win. Every time the team loses, he feels it deeply. Losing is the worst thing in the world to him because he's just too passionate about the game. While that passion is appreciated, his feelings of loss become all-encompassing. It can often set him back. If he's too focused on the loss, he can't pay attention to the next play or how to work with the team to make improvements. He needs to learn that loss and failure offer teachable moments.

We can't focus on our losses, otherwise we won't move forward and grow. Many successful people have gotten where they are because they experienced loss and grew from it. They learned from their failures and applied those lessons to their next venture. Not every business you touch will turn to gold, but what you learn from failure is just as valuable as what you gain from success.

This shift in our mindset is crucial. It's easy for people to experience loss and then immediately point their fingers elsewhere. They point to an event, a person, a company, a government, anything. They point to anything that is outside of them. Pointing the finger somewhere else won't help you get over the loss and you'll lose focus on fixing the problem. You'll be bitter and blame the world, capitalism, or whatever outside force led you to that failure. The loss will sit with you until you finally let it go.

In my situation, I could have easily blamed the recession, the government, the housing bubble, whoever. And maybe a part of me did. But I also took the next step to reflect and see how I contributed to my own loss.

Reflection is essential in moving past a loss. I like to take that pointing finger and redirect it at myself. What could I have done better to make this situation a win, instead of a loss? What could I do better next time? What could I learn from this? What can I do right now to start fixing things? In my reflection, I found that ego led me to my massive growth, as well as my massive fall. I wasn't paying attention to the market. This is something I could fix for the next time, and there would be a next time.

This mindset shift is often called a fixed-to-growth mindset. These terms have been pretty popular for a couple of years now. A fixed mindset is where you believe you can't change and that your choices and actions are based entirely on talent or special skill. A growth mindset is one where you know you can change, grow from your circumstances, and ultimately learn from your failures.

In a fixed mindset, you are set on a path to eventually fail and never bounce back. If you fail with a fixed mindset, you dwell on that and point the fingers anywhere else. You're more likely to become defensive when you identify that you've made a mistake. You're so busy protecting your ego, that you can't learn from your failure.

On the other hand, a growth mindset sets us up to succeed. It helps people like you and me recognize that we are constantly growing and learning. We're capable of resilience and learning from our mistakes. A growth mindset is what we need to succeed in business and life. It sets us up for goal planning and development.

A part of growth mindset is learning to reflect on what went wrong. If people acknowledged what they could do better, they would be able to move on and find a quicker solution.

Focus on Solutions

As I said earlier, I'm a solution-oriented person. I want to identify the problem and learn from my mistakes. After identifying, reflecting, and learning, I know I can start moving on. I can't stay in the same place and sit with the loss any longer. I need to take the steps to move forward and build momentum. If I can get momentum going, I can find a way out of stagnant moments.

An easy way to start building momentum is to look for quick wins. By this, I mean getting something done right now. It can be something simple and not too time-consuming. If I have a to-do list, I'll complete three or four quick things on it that won't take up much of my time. By checking these things off my list, I am moving forward and building momentum.

I like to use my morning routine as a good example. After waking up, you could jump immediately into work. But really, that's a big step. Instead, take the small wins. Get out of bed. Brush your teeth. Eat breakfast. Enjoy some coffee. Read a little. Then move over to your desk. Read your to-do list for the day. And get started. There. Momentum. Start with the small steps instead of the big ones, and keep pushing forward.

We can't move forward if we're trapped in the past or too worried about the future. Dwelling on past mistakes or feeling fretful over future moves only gets you stuck in the mud. If we look at a business loss as an unsolvable problem, then we stop moving. Focusing on the problem and sitting in it only makes it grow. It becomes an overbearing mountain that we have to deal with instead of the small molehill it used to be. Instead of focusing on the loss, focus on the solutions. If you focus on the problem, it only gets bigger and you'll have a harder time building the momentum to overcome it. If you focus on finding a solution, the problem becomes easier to deal with. So focus on the solution.

Do this by looking at a problem and asking yourself how you can fix it. This problem is fixable, as most problems are. So, how can we overcome it? It's a puzzle to solve, not an insurmountable challenge. If we break a problem down into much smaller steps, we can solve smaller issues. We can build the momentum and confidence to keep solving smaller problems. This ultimately moves us towards tackling the larger ones.

Now, you may think that the end goal is to be problem-free. But that's neither realistic nor achievable. Instead, I challenge you to look forward to your problems. Having a problem means you are growing and learning, or at least getting the opportunity to do so. It means you're not coasting. The bigger problems you solve, the more your company can grow.

We can either be solution-oriented or have a growth mindset. We're not restricted by one type and can develop the skills to move forward. Any skill can be learned and developed. One skill I had to take the time to grow was my leadership skills, especially when it was time to delegate tasks. It's a tough skill to learn and when you want to control all of the little details, it can be a struggle.

By developing the skills to become a better entrepreneur, I become a better leader for my team. Learning and growing from your problems is easier with a growth mindset. Everything can be learned; you just have to identify what needs to be improved. You start by acknowledging the loss or problem, and then taking the steps to find a solution.

While I am eager to find solutions for all my problems, some are not mine to solve. Similarly, you cannot know everything, so some are for others to know. During the Great Recession, my attorneys had to solve some of the legal and financial problems that resulted from losing the company. I didn't have the means to solve these problems on my own, nor did I know everything about the law. Not being able to solve a problem on your own is not a weakness. It just means that you're human and not all-knowing. And there's probably someone else out there with the experience, education, or means, to help you.

I like to be the problem solver in my work (and possibly in your work too). I'm a natural problem solver. I have the experience, education, and means to solve most if not all marketing problems. Because of this, a client will come to me with very specific marketing problems and I can help them solve it. You cannot solve all of your problems on your own. No man is an island, and sometimes a problem needs to be addressed by a team. You have to recognize when a problem is beyond your control. As an entrepreneur, you think you can do it all, but the fact is that you can't. You have to learn when it's time to hand off the problem to someone else who is more able to solve it. Don't stop and sit in the problem. Indecision is already a bad decision.

HIT THE GAS

What are some losses you've experienced?

___

How can you use them to better plan for wins?

___

"The difference between average people and achieving people is their perception of and response to failure."

John C. Maxwell

Chapter 3

Do Less

    This is connected to our previous discussion on not being able to solve all of your problems. Sometimes, you have to hand problems off to someone else and hope for the best. So many people try to do everything on their own and I was one of those people. I would work in the trenches doing absolutely everything for my business. If someone called me, I micromanaged everything that resulted from the call. I wanted to be in control of everything because it was my business and I had worked hard to create it. I had to learn that some people are more capable of dealing with things than I am.

    Everything I did in my business had to be 100% perfect. Do you know how draining that is? It's impossible to make everything perfect but I would try my hardest. Then I realized if I could put someone in place who did about 75% of what I would do, then that's still a win. And everything is still okay. I had to learn how to delegate because I was exhausting myself to the bone trying to get everything done (and done perfectly).

After a certain point, a business owner needs to change the way they work. You should be doing less of the little things and focus on the bigger things. It's your job to lead, not just be in the trenches slaving away the whole time. When you're trying to do it all, you're restricting yourself, your team, and your company. If you've hired well, then the people who work with you are more than capable of doing their jobs effectively, They feel confident about the work they do, without you having to micromanage everything.

This was a difficult lesson for me. It's hard to build a business, something that you care for a lot, and then hand it over to others. In my first business, I created an environment where my team had to ask for permission to do anything. Everything that was going on needed my approval. I got so frustrated with them asking me questions they should've been able to answer themselves. I thought they could do this, so why are they coming to me? I then realized I had set up this environment. I made them ask me the questions and come to me for executive decisions. I had created a situation where everyone was working with one hand tied behind their backs. It was unsupportive.

Because I wanted to be in control of everything, my company stopped growing. While there weren't any losses, we didn't make any gains either. I created an environment where my team members were not happy with the work. If I wanted a growing company with happier employees, then I needed to make some changes.

I had to empower my team and create processes that were easy to duplicate. This way, my team could handle it with their own expertise and then train others on it. It also left me free to do what I needed in the business. I had to ask what others could take care of and what was required of me.

I started down that path with new clients. New clients didn't know that I'd micromanaged everything before, so I passed them along to my team. My team knew how to operate. They could handle more of the work, and I could micromanage less. I had set up a better system.

My team and I have learned to delegate, so that we're always streamlining the process. At this point, the team is smarter about the process than I am. I'm just there to guide it and help them grow. Sometimes you have to take a step back to get things moving forward. This move led to a happier workforce and each person was working within their expertise instead of relying on me to tell them what to do. They aren't grinding away and stressed by the work, but satisfied with it. The other benefit is more growth in the company.

ALL GAS, NO BRAKES

During this process, I lost money. I was taking a step back from our normal routine to establish a new one and revenue went down, I lost or either let go of clients, and took a major hit. After the transition was complete and I set up a new system, revenue went further than ever before. It quickly bounced back and exceeded what I imagined.

I think people struggle with doing less because of ego. We want to control everything, and to say that we did it on our own. But we have to accept help from others who are capable of handling things for us. Just like the financial attorneys, sometimes a problem isn't ours to solve. In this case, I had to give control to my employees who had the expertise and the means to handle things without my oversight. But giving up control means that I was able to do less busy work and focus more on my role within the agency.

People are also hesitant to do less because of revenue. That is the only metric they are focused on. And most people won't do the streamlining process if it's a dip in revenue. If a company is paying you so much money a month, you may be willing to just sit with it, even if your business and employees are struggling. For us, we had to think about how to make the transition without giving up money. In the end, we just bit the bullet and transitioned to the new process. Within a year, we made massive growth in revenue. It's scary making pivots in your business, but if you believe you're headed in the right direction, it's worth it.

Doing less was also important to me. I was choosing a lifestyle over money, which was important because I've always wanted to be there for my family. By doing less, and micromanaging less, I was able to spend more time with my family. I didn't have to work all of the time. It also made me more present with my family. I didn't have to constantly put out fires, or check my messages to see how things were going. I could enjoy family time without worrying about business decisions or if a client was being left in the lurch. Doing less meant that I could focus more on what mattered to me, in both business and my personal life.

Do the Work

When I started doing less, I had to identify what work I was going to do less of. The thing is: I was busy being busy. In business, we are always putting out fires or have a mindless list of things to get done. I was doing all of these things, but it was work someone else could've been doing. I should have been focused on becoming a better leader, empowering my team, and creating strategies for growth. Instead, I was building funnels, creating ad copy, or going through a to-do list that someone else could have easily done. It was a grind to get through everything.

There is a difference between unproductive work and productive work. For me, answering emails, micromanaging, and building funnels was unproductive and no longer needed. Productive work would have been focusing on the future of the business. It's important to recognize that difference. Are you doing productive work that fits your role, or are you doing unproductive work someone else could be doing?

When you're a business owner, you have to be careful about the work you're doing. Don't get me wrong, when you're starting you're going to be doing most of the work yourself. Once you're established, you should be more careful about the work you're choosing to do. If you're still doing everything in your business a year later, then you need to find ways to level up your work and transfer the busy tasks to someone else. If you're not leveling up the kind of work you're doing, then you're staying stagnant.

Leveling up your work means moving from creating ad copy and building funnels to focusing on leadership skills. This is a change in the work that I was already doing in my agency. I hired people to create ad copy and build funnels while I focused on leadership skills. So level up your work.

When transitioning the company, I had to see what my employees could do and where they should be focused. An important part of this is making sure everyone knows what their role is. A team should always know what work they're focusing on, and this includes the boss (you!). This didn't come easy for me, and it took a long time to execute it within my own company. But defining the roles for everyone made it easier to create meaningful work and do less of the daily grind activities.

Without defining the clear-cut work, we end up on a grind, just doing all the little tasks and putting out fires. We grow frustrated with our work and the company. We end up jumping in and micromanaging the team because we don't know what people are supposed to be doing. You'll get a crazy amount of turnover when people leave to find more fulfilling work. Without defined results, people won't know what they're trying to accomplish. People want to be successful in the work they do, so without clear goals, how will they be successful?

Without clarity, team members become resentful. It can create an environment that's toxic for everyone and make a miserable work experience. You can create a good environment by having clear roles and making sure people are using their expertise in the right areas. If you hire people based on clearly defined results and work they're good at, you'll have created an opportunity for someone to enjoy working with you. They'll have pride in the work they do.

HIT THE GAS

What work can you pass off to someone else? What could you do less of?

_____
_____
_____
_____
_____
_____
_____

What do you want to be most focused on?

_____
_____
_____
_____
_____
_____
_____

"Talent wins games, but teamwork and intelligence win championships."

Michael Jordan

Chapter 4

Empower Your Team

      This goes hand in hand with the previous chapter about stepping back from doing everything, while ensuring that everyone is doing the work they should be. When I started my company, I created it knowing that I was an expert. I knew how to do everything by myself and if I didn't know something, I figured it out. In my eyes, I was always the best at doing everything. This, of course, wasn't true, but it's how I felt at the time. I wanted to be in control of everything and it was the mindset that led me to micromanaging everything. It's hard to empower your team if you're doing everything yourself.

      Whenever a problem came up, I always jumped in to solve it instead of letting my team figure it out. It weakened the team's confidence in being able to problem solve and take accountability for their work. There was no reassurance of their value within the team. Because of this, I had a lot of turnover in the company and people left to find more fulfilling work. I should have empowered my team to make decisions because they were more than capable of doing that.

As entrepreneurs and leaders, we have to motivate our team and encourage them to make decisions. We have to let them take responsibility and handle difficult situations. We all take pride in our work, but stepping in to make the decisions all the time sends the message: "I don't trust you to solve this problem yourself." It's incredibly demeaning. We have to let go of the control so that our team does what they were hired to do.

This sounds like such an easy concept, but it took me a long time to learn. Six years ago, I hired someone to be the COO when my agency was growing. He had a lot of management experience but not as much in marketing. I ended up trying to let him run everything and manage people. I let him make decisions for the company and cut back on my work in an attempt to do less. Then I would come back and undercut him in front of the team, instead of trusting his decisions.

We all have an ego and as an entrepreneur, it might be a little larger than others. In this situation, my ego led me to undercut this man I had hired. Subconsciously, I was saying that I was the boss and knew what was right. I wasn't ready to let go of control and tried to put him on a leash. Everyone saw that it caused issues and it created a toxic work environment.

The COO wasn't ever able to lead properly because I didn't empower him. I didn't build him up and acknowledge what he did in front of the team. I didn't even really set him up properly with the team, I just brought him in off the street and told everyone he was in charge.

Part of this mistake was made out of inexperience. I didn't know how to create a more empowering environment for my team or have the skills to successfully set someone up. I had to work on my leadership skills to make sure it didn't happen again. I learned a lot on how to motivate people and put them in the right position to succeed.

Your team needs a sense of control that they're making valuable decisions. They need a sense of belonging to the community and an acknowledgment of their contributions. The team needs to see themselves as part of the success of the company (because they are!). I want them to see a future with this company, where they grow and learn with us.

The first need of our teams is a sense of control in decision-making. It's natural to hold onto the reigns of a company you've created, but you need the buy-in from a team. While I care so much about the company, I have to remember that my colleagues also care. They want to see the company succeed. And while that success can be tied to me, it's important to empower employees so that they put their all into the work.

We can create a sense of control by creating very clear roles in the workplace. If people know exactly what's expected of them, then they're more likely to feel in control of what's happening in their workday. They never have to guess if they're doing the right or wrong thing, or ask for permission to do their work. During our transition, creating clearer roles for the company led to more focused work with a happier team. There was less stress grinding through the day. Knowing the full scope of your job and being reassured that it fits within your expertise immediately gives people the confidence in the work and ability to complete it.

Another way we empower our teams is to build a sense of belonging to the community. This can be done in many different ways, but one of them is to show regular care to each team member. Get to know them and who they are. They have lives outside of work and are more than just valuable team members.

It's important to recognize how much work they're putting in, and then encouraging them to take breaks and care for themselves too. As entrepreneurs, we're encouraged to hustle and work 24/7. We often push those working for us to do the same. There's a time and place for hustling, but you can't expect others to dedicate that time. They have their own lives to pursue and take care of.

I try to encourage my employees to take their time off. We're all driven and want to see the same results, but we've also got life outside of work. And a well-balanced life is no joke. It's important not to overwork your team, as it often leads to burn-out, reduction in creativity, higher turnover, and a miserable group of people. If team members take time off, they often come back recharged and ready to work again.

    Finally, acknowledging work well done is an essential way to empower your team. Acknowledgment reminds your team that their contributions are valued and they are appreciated. It reminds them of what they did well and improves their confidence in getting things done. I have made a focused effort to encourage others and point out what they've done well, rather than what they didn't do. Acknowledge the work that people are doing for you and the company. It can be fulfilling, but also help them recognize their worth within the company.

    Motivating your team is an ongoing effort. Learning how to be a good leader is a skill that has to constantly be developed. There's never a set benchmark for that, so you have to keep working on it.

NATE KENNEDY

The other day we elevated a team member into more of a leadership role. She got an email from a client who was unhappy about something, and I started writing back to the client. Right before I clicked send, I realized I should reach out and ask her how she wanted to respond. She gave me her breakdown of what she wanted to do and I gave her feedback on the message. She sent it off and it went well. I congratulated her and asked her to lead this part of the company, adding that I trust her opinion and decision-making.

The result was so positive for her and the company because I'm learning more about what it means to empower others and be a good leader. I'm not perfect after all, I nearly sent that email myself. But I am always working on it.

HIT THE GAS

In what ways are you disempowering your team?

_____
_____
_____
_____
_____
_____
_____

Now, what can you do to empower them?

_____
_____
_____
_____
_____
_____
_____

"Surround yourself with those who want you to succeed. People who don't pursue their own dreams won't encourage you to pursue yours."

Tim Grover

Chapter 5

Don't Seek Counsel from False Prophets

When you enter the world of entrepreneurship and commence on your unique journey, you are bound to come across other competitors, entrepreneurs, and business people. Each one of them will have their own personalized goals, ventures, abilities, perspectives, and above all, their respective level of ego. Make no mistake – this world is significantly more competitive than you might imagine. Everyone around you will start to boast just how important they are. If you made a million dollars last year, they would come up to you and say, "Well, I made twice as much." Well, good for you.

It is just absurd and fairly childish to get into the comparison game. Most people who highlight their importance are bluffing. Here is a rule of thumb; a successful person will never enter the comparison game, period. Those who continue to flaunt their so-called "success," let them do so. Do not be deterred, and do not let their words make you feel awful. I assure you; you are doing far better than them.

It doesn't take long for young entrepreneurs to learn the kind of people they should hang around with and those they should avoid. There is no "one-size-fits-all" solution here, and that means that you will need to use your intuition to figure that out.

I used to go to various masterminds every year. I wanted to meet different people, get to know them, and learn from them.

Masterminds are a great place to share your ideas, get feedback, and surround yourself with A-Players.

To anyone, that may seem like a perfectly logical thing to do. It would also make sense if I say that everyone at these events was good at giving fruitful advice, right? Well, no!

Advice – On the House!

When I say "false prophets," I am labeling a few types of people who claim to know it all. They only go on to tell you things that would harm you instead. I came across some of these people at events. While there were many successful entrepreneurs, some were just advising for the sake of it. They were giving away their opinions based on the feeling to do so, not because they had done or experienced the same thing.

Would you ask an engineer for a medical opinion? It doesn't make any sense to do so. Yet people often seek advice from others who have never done the same thing.

Everyone loves advising because it makes them feel special and heard. It is just how our mind works. However, this does not mean that every piece of advice you get will be productive, meaningful, or even accurate. Be very careful of the people who just love to hand out advice. They'll try to tell you how to conduct your business, why you should avoid investing in something, or how you should aim to do X, Y, and Z, just because they believe it is worth doing. If that is the case, why aren't they doing it themselves?

I was once discussing a business plan with a group of people when I distinctively remember a guy who approached me. I was hoping to share my ideas and get meaningful tips, in an attempt to make my business plan better. I was already given a tip by my friend and mentor, who was quite specific with his words. He said, "Do not change your business path based on the advice you received in these masterminds."

This is quite true. Everyone has a lens through which they view the world. If you are someone who does not like the idea of investing in stocks, then you will always tell the world not to do so either. You could miss out on a lot of the goodness that stocks may hold, but you'll only be able to filter out things that are meaningful to you. Similarly, some people will come up to you, telling you how you are mistaken, and how things will not work out the way you want them to. Just remember, they are only viewing things through their unique lenses. You just need to find someone who shares the same lens as you.

When you go on to change your business, you let go of your vision. You might come up with a new business idea that others like, but it may not line up with your core values. This clash would see that you fail, and fail miserably. Okay, back to the story here.

After listening to my offer, a guy approached me and started to belittle me. His ego was taking over as he started sharing his opinions on my business idea. I consider myself a quiet person and do not normally react or speak much, but there came a point where I was no longer able to hear him continue. I looked at him and couldn't help myself from asking, "Who are you?"

In all honesty, that wasn't what I said, but I am sure you can imagine the kind of words I used. It certainly surprised everyone around me. Some were even shocked to see me react that way. Then the person ever-so-confidently told me, "You will be out of business in the next year." He was not only handing me over bad advice and telling me what 'not' to do, but also how I would end up losing it all. The product that I was highlighting, which deemed 'useless,' went on to generate $1 million in revenue in just two months. Needless to say, it went tremendously.

Some people will listen to you, guide you accordingly, and expect nothing in return except to see you succeed. Then, there are guys like him. These are the kind of people who will never have your best interests in mind. They would only disappoint you and make you feel inferior while trying to boast just how successful and incomparable they are. Never seek out advice from those who do not have the experience to back it up. Never listen to the naysayers either.

Taking a Leap of Faith

At another mastermind, my partner and I wanted to talk about a company product and get some advice on it. Back in the day, everyone was about Google Ads and Facebook Ads. No one was talking about funnels and working in the marketing space. I wanted to build a funnel company with my partner. I was the tech guy and my partner was the copywriter; it was a perfect match.

This was four years before click funnels software ever rolled out. We were putting this together and started selling projects. When we went to mastermind to get advice on how to grow the business, we were told we shouldn't do it. That it wasn't a "good fit" for us and we should try something else.

My partner and I were so dejected and frustrated, as it wasn't the response we were looking for. We bounced back and decided to ditch the advice and create the business anyway. We pushed forward and did well with it. One month later, we were competing with the exact same guys who told us not to start the business in the first place. Ironic, isn't it? It turned out that they were creating a similar business. They already had the pieces in play and a large client list to work with. They had their business in the works when they told us ours wouldn't work. And they didn't tell us we would be competing during the mastermind call. This was a potential motivator for why they gave us the advice they did.

My recommendation is to always be cautious with the advice you receive from masterminds or entrepreneurs you don't know very well. Consider their underlying motives and remember that they are only hearing or seeing something partial, not the full picture. Try to understand where they're coming from and why they're giving you the advice they are.

Getting good advice is about having mentors that you can turn to. We'll talk more about this in a later chapter, but for now, having a mentor means having someone who is knowledgeable in your arena and will be able to provide you with quality advice.

My recommendation for choosing good mentors is to find someone who has already done something similar to what you want to accomplish. Find mentors who are in the same field, not just entrepreneurs in miscellaneous areas. When I started as a marketer I looked for mentors with marketing experience. As I evolved as a CEO and Investor, I started looking for different mentors. I wanted to ask the right questions to the right people. This is the only way to know you're getting good information.

The more clear you are about yourself and what you are looking for, the easier it will be to find mentors who fit your values. Mentors who will give you quality advice and share your passion. You'll know who to avoid, as they're not pursuing similar things as you or having values that match yours.

Clarity plays a vital role in your business, and life in general. It is through having clarity that you can decide where you want to go in life. Then you are able to define a clear path from here to there, something many entrepreneurs end up failing at. For a good part of their careers, they go on experimenting with a variety of ideas before eventually figuring out. "Ah, man! How did we miss that?" By that time, most of the opportunities are gone.

If you are someone who is still struggling with ideas, my recommendation is to first gain clarity on what you truly want to pursue. It could be a business model, a lifestyle, writing a book, or anything else. Do not try to move ahead with a vague idea as you would not be prepared for what you might come across. It would consume more time, and the results may not be satisfactory.

One of the hardest parts of being an entrepreneur is figuring out who we are and what we want. Once we've got that down, we can start to build a business that supports our growth. Most of the time, we don't go deep enough on our desires. We stay vague about what we want. We say "I just want a good business" or "I want to be happy." But that's not really deep or even specific into what you want. It's a tough question and hard to answer. It's also an answer that will frequently change over time. What I wanted at 25 is not what I want now. Getting a clear picture of what you want sets the path to follow. Life will change your desires, and you may

Go to NateKennedy.com/allgas for a raw, uncut video I recorded for entrepreneurs that want to have Lifestyle Freedom.

pivot to something else, but you have to ultimately know what you want.

Once you know what you want and value, it's easier to find the mentors and people who give quality advice. It takes time to develop that group of people, but you can always start with one person, and grow from there.

My approach to masterminds have also changed. I stopped going to them for the tactics and advice. I started going for the relationships and have built my small yet strong circle of great people.

NATE KENNEDY

HIT THE GAS

In what ways do you compare your success to others?

_____
_____
_____
_____
_____
_____
_____

How can you be more focused on your success, your wants, your values?

_____
_____
_____
_____
_____
_____
_____

> *"Success is not final; failure is not fatal: it is the courage to continue that counts."*
>
> **Winston Churchill**

Chapter 6

Decisions, Decisions

We have all been guilty of making decisions based purely off our emotions. Whether it was to invest in a trendy business we feel 'lucky' about or to stop approaching contacts who do not respond at all, we have all made decisions driven by emotion. Let's pause here for a minute and reflect a little; how many of those decisions turned out to be right? Mind you; these are not based on any data at all.

I can confidently say that the answer many would have come up with would be 'few' or 'none.' But responding with emotion is only natural. Even if those decisions drag us into more troublesome situations. Most of us have egos riding with us, and that ego often interferes. It sends you down a different path than the one intended. We end up making bad decisions and are later left to face the music.

Now let's change that a little and introduce a bit of data into the mix. Every success story you come across has this fantastic ability to avoid drama and focus solely on the data. They have mastered the ability to block their emotions and let the numbers do the talking. They go on to break records. Why? Because the data never introduces drama; it only shows what is and what can be. Some of the decisions may tough. Your data might suggest that you lay someone off that you liked working with. But if that person isn't productive enough, they are a liability, and liabilities must go. Take these steps and I assure you; you will be achieving success unlike ever before.

Learning All About Data

Let's assume you have a wonderful idea that will surely work wonders. You are all excited to discuss the idea with someone and get positive feedback. You start to dig in and explore it further, just to see how profitable the idea will be. You do all of that without reflecting on the data, knowing that this idea is just too good to pass. You go all-in.

A few months down the road and the feeling of uneasiness starts to creep up to you. You remain positive that the results will come, still overlooking the importance of data. A few more months go by and you're at a point where you're ready to either give up or reassess your idea. Certainly, you have already invested a significant period, and giving up now would seem illogical. You have an expert go through the data and end up finding out that the idea was anything but good. The numbers don't add up and you can only expect to make enough to recover your investment. That's it. While you could've experienced worse, all of the positivity and vibes you had for the idea has vanished. If you had only looked at the data when you had the chance.

Today, we live in a data-driven world where you can maximize your chances of success. If you are launching a product, you can reverse engineer the numbers that support it to show whether revenue would be coming in or out. Only then are you to move forward with the idea. You can do this with a spreadsheet and basic financial modeling, yet a lot of entrepreneurs avoid it. The data, especially today, is your friend. It acknowledges what works and what doesn't. It also supports the decision-making process for the rest of your life. I learned that from @MarkEvansDM.

Through the use of data, you can discover critical pieces of information such as:

- How many clients you will need to generate, the kind of revenue you are targeting, per day, per week, month and year.
- When you will hit your breakeven point
- How much you should price your product
- What kind of profit you can expect over the next quarter or year
- How many leads are needed to get moving

Based on these important pieces of information, you can decide whether the model is something to work with or not. This is just the start.

@MarkEvansDM taught me the importance of relying on the data, not drama. Those are his words and his phrasing, so I have to give him a shoutout for this chapter, and frankly many chapters in this book.

We make many decisions in business, but we have to make sure we're making those decisions from the right perspective. It comes down to making decisions based on logic, not emotions. This is something I've done a lot in the past, and something we all do. You get super excited about working on an idea, just to step back and realize it wasn't going to make you any money. You have to look at the data and know if the numbers are going to work out. For a business to work, what do the numbers have to look like?

What does the data have to flow like in order to create a profitable business? A business only works when you're focused on the data.

However, a lot of people run a business based on emotions and tend to skip over the steps of running a financial model. The financial model lets you rely on the data and get a clearer picture of what you're hoping to accomplish. Breaking down a business idea into its various data points gets the clearest idea of what we're doing. So break it down into how many clients, leads, etc. It's a whole process, but it gives you an idea of how the business will turn out.

When we're starting with a new business idea, it's easy to get fired up and make decisions based on our gut. It's an instinctive decision and not a data-driven decision. With bubbling feelings of excitement, it's easy to get carried away and create a business that sounds great in theory, but terrible in practice.

As a marketer, you have paid traffic, sales funnel, and a certain matrix with every step. These can include your cost per click, the conversion rate on the landing page, cost per lead, the cost for having a sales call, and so much more. Having this data allows you to make smart decisions and take actions that will generate you revenue, and ultimately success.

ALL GAS, NO BRAKES

  I use an internal sheet with all the data points to make decisions. When I look at these numbers, I can identify the weaknesses and take whatever action is necessary.

  A lot of people tend to go on their gut feelings. They end up making a few emotional decisions, and in a few months later, end up in a completely different direction than the one they originally intended. This is also true when people copy business practices and decisions. Just because it's "working out for them," doesn't mean the same for you. The exact same practices and methods that worked for someone else could bring your business to the brink of bankruptcy. People's emotions get the better of their judgment, and what may shine isn't always gold. A model that works successfully for someone else may not fetch me, or you, the same kind of success. There is a lot more that goes on behind the curtains, and people tend to overlook those matters.

  We only get to see the professionally painted picture and are amused easily. To us, it would feel like "Wow! I am doing that as well." All the chaotic matters that take place behind the scenes are neither advertised nor made public, and for good reasons too. If these matters were to find themselves open to the public, almost every business in existence will go down. People will end up losing their investor's trust, see their stocks fall, and most certainly struggle to gain a new client moving forward. That part of the story remains hidden, and most of us tend to overlook that aspect. It is only after we apply these methods that we realize just how insane the problems are, but by then, it would already be too late.

To summarize, emotional decisions are best left outside the door. There is simply no room for emotions or emotion-based decisions in the world of entrepreneurship. Always look at the data. The numbers will never lie to you, even when your emotions might. Look at what your numbers are reflecting, and then proceed towards making the kind of decision that help you move forward.

They Only Tell You Their Gains

By now, it would be fairly easy to figure out that people have this great tendency of revealing parts of the information while retaining the other. In these masterminds, I have come across a dozen success stories and how they've had the best results. Sure, it eventually came for most of them, but that does not mean it was smooth sailing the entire time. They often go on to highlight a single day of the entire quarter, and that single day is essentially their best. They received significant results, and to them, that is the highlight of their marketing campaign. They go on talking about how they were able to do this and achieve that, but are never able to share the hardships they had to face, just to make it where they are today.

It is just like how Instagram works. You might have the toughest day of your life or feel stressed about something, but one good picture uploaded would show the rest of the world how you are leading a perfect life. They would never realize just how depressed or troubled you may be. To them, seeing is believing, and they are only seeing things as they appear, not how they truly are.

Every marketing campaign you initiate will be shrouded with doubts, questions, problems, and consequences. Allowing your emotions to take the lead does not guarantee good results, even if someone at as mastermind said it helped them hit their targets easily. You are not guaranteed the same results. If the numbers don't add up, you are headed towards an imminent failure. Your data is your biggest asset, and I see the same being the case for generations to come. We have stepped out of the era where data was only secondary. Today, the data will help get going in any field, and in any direction that you want.

Data-based Decisions – The Way Forward

Making data-driven decisions is not only important when starting a venture, but also when continuing to grow a business. This is especially true when addressing problems or issues that come up. It's very easy to freak out when a problem arises and make drama-based decisions. Following your gut to solve a problem may completely miss the mark because you didn't look at the data, or what created the problem in the first place.

An emotional response is the stagnation we discussed earlier. Just sitting there and dwelling on the problem is the same as throwing in the towel and calling it a day. And while it's okay to throw in the towel, make sure that decision is based on the data, and less on a spur of the moment decision.

With the data right in front of you, you know where the problem is or where the business can grow. It's not just a gut feeling or based on any emotions.

In marketing, data over drama has become even more relevant. Marketing is emotional in the sense that your goal is to connect with the client and bring them into your selling arena. So it can be dramatic, and it can work slowly or quickly, depending on so many factors. A lot of people will look at a marketing campaign after day one and claim that it sucked because there was no immediate return. That response can lead them to scrap the whole thing entirely based on temporary emotions. And maybe the campaign did work. If we look at the data, maybe it shows a different story. Or if they wait a bit longer, the campaign could work for them. All gas and no brakes, right? Emotional decisions can end something too early, or start something too late, all without paying attention to the data.

If you are getting into online marketing, do not get frustrated if your campaign is not working the way you want it to. You are in the same boat as everybody else, and the sooner you accept that, the easier it will be. You will no longer feel the necessity to immediately validate your efforts. You will no longer be drawn to the idea of scoring a win on every marketing campaign because truth is told, no one can do that either.

This struck me right on time. I was leading a team and in the same phase feeling frustrated with my campaigns and the results I wanted. After realizing that others go through the same thing, it helped me feel a lot better and allowed me to focus my efforts more constructively.

If you ever have the chance to talk to a major marketing entrepreneur, you will learn that they are happy if they can have two or three of their 10 offers work for them. These are guys who make serious money and generate massive revenues. This is contrary to popular belief, but it is true. Those who claim to hit eight or nine times out of 10 are either trying to show themselves to be something they are not, or trying to fool you into thinking you are not good.

NATE KENNEDY

"If you are interviewing a copywriter who claims to have all victories, hire someone else!"

I learned that every campaign is not a winning campaign. Of course, I did not want to start from scratch every time, because it is far too cumbersome. All of the marketing campaigns I work on have a variety of touch points to utilize and better my craft. I ask, "how do I identify where the hole is?" and use data to figure things out. Data has allowed me to fine-tune my designs, proposals, and offers.

There are a few KPIs that you should keep in mind and focus on.

1. Figure out the cost per client acquisition.
2. Figure out the customer cart value
3. Find out the customer's lifetime value

Let's say that it costs $1000 to acquire a customer, but my average customer value is $2500. For every customer I draw in, I end up making $1500. That makes sense and I have the data to support that. The numbers add up and are pointing the right way. Making a decision is a lot easier when I know how much I would end up making, how much time it would take, and how long I expect the customer to do business with me. All of these key performance indicators (KPIs) will be in the compiled data and provides a path to follow. Once the guesswork is sorted out, I can make all of the decisions I need based on the data.

Recalibrate Your Focus

Focusing on the data instead of the drama is very important when you're struggling to make a new business decision. If you're struggling to make a decision, trust the numbers. Numbers don't lie.

People often focus on the revenue they want to generate on their very first day. If there isn't any, they believe the business model is set up to fail. That is neither true nor a reality. The first day would often go blank. But instead of limiting your focus to the first day, look at the bigger picture. Yes, the client you attracted might have cost you $1000, and they may only return $800 by the end of the month, but the same customer may generate $2500 in the next 30 days, followed by $5000 in the third month. Allow your data to figure matters out and tell the real story.

It is a general rule of thumb that those who spend the most to acquire a customer will be able to take the business from those who are unwilling. It is something that I have always believed to be true and have followed the same idea myself. Needless to say, I can see those who overlook or undermine the same concept. They are struggling to even keep their ships afloat, let alone sailing smoothly.

If you know your data, you will know the lifetime values of a customer. Based on that information, you can confidently invest money and drive traffic to your business.

Getting it Wrong!

I have seen people looking at data and using it all wrong. This often leads them to question why they should trust the data alone in the first place. But the numbers cannot lie, and if you still end up making the wrong decisions, there is bound to be something else wrong.

One of the most common things that I have seen is people focusing on far too many data points. The more there are, the easier it is to confuse yourself. However, that isn't even the biggest problem here; it is trying too many things at once.

When you start doing a lot of things at once, you will never learn how one affects the other. You will never come to realize the true effect or impact that any of these things may have on your business, whether positive or negative. It will certainly increase cost, and it will not allow you to know what is harming your business and what is strengthening it.

Let's say that you decide to change the headline on your landing page, the layout of the navigation menu, and the way an email is sent out. You are already doing too much. How on earth will you figure out what is working and what isn't? There is no clear way to know unless you try each of these things, one thing at a time. Change one thing, wait for the results to pour in, and review the data. Your data will reveal if this generates more business or costs you money. If it worked, keep it and improve upon it. If not, stick with the control. You may feel emotionally driven to add a button, or update the layout just because you came across something that excited you, but know that it may not work for the kind of business you are doing.

Having an emotional response is not necessarily a bad thing. After all, we have gut feelings for a reason. If you have an emotional response, back it up with data first. While some entrepreneurs have killer gut instincts and pick good ventures based on their gut, it's still a good idea to back that up with the data so that your decision has a more secure foundation.

HIT THE GAS

Evaluate how you make decisions. What's your process?

_____
_____
_____
_____
_____
_____
_____

How can you ensure that you remain open to change, if and when needed?

_____
_____
_____
_____
_____
_____
_____

"Often any decision, even the wrong decision, is better than no decision."

Ben Horowitz

Chapter 7

Don't Stop Marketing

Talk about an emotional decision. The moment that shit hits the fan in a business, quick decisions are being made. People start looking at their finances and trying to find somewhere to make their dollars stretch a bit further.

I've talked to so many business owners throughout the years and when things get tough, the first thing they cut is their marketing budget. Marketing and sales are like chicken and egg, what comes first? At the end of the day, marketing, to me, is the front-end system that allows you to generate sales on the back end. Marketing matters and ,without it, you don't have anyone to sell to.

A lot of people think that the money put into marketing can be easily put elsewhere. And it can be, but will it be as effective? Marketing is the means of spreading your business, especially in times of financial difficulties. Money can easily be put elsewhere, but without marketing, how are you going to attract the attention to keep your business afloat in tough times? If your revenue is off for the month, why would you stop marketing? Why would you not try to generate more clients?

Many people choose to cut marketing budgets because they're focused on the drama of the situation, instead of the data that supports them. If you understand the data of what's going in and out, then you also understand the revenue being generated by your marketing campaigns. It's a no-brainer (and worth keeping).

Instead of cutting marketing budgets, get smarter with your marketing and never stop. Businesses want to dip their toes into every kind of online marketing they can get their hands on. They just start putting out more and more things. They market through Facebook, YouTube, Google Ads, SEO, you name it. But when these companies have a bad month, they cut off all the marketing completely and redistribute the funds. They should be looking at the sources driving the revenue and invest more. You can pinpoint the areas turning the most profitable sales and market smarter. You don't have to market harder or stop altogether.

There is no denying that 2020 has been a very difficult year for businesses. Because of the pandemic, many were hit with financial hardships and looking to cut costs. Expenditures and marketing budgets are often the first to go. And most businesses make these decisions without looking at the data.

I chose to do the opposite. I know that this is only a cycle and that people will eventually be back in business and looking to expand. I put everything into marketing my business. We grew. I knew revenue was going down, but I also knew that I shouldn't stop marketing. I decided to keep putting money into it because I believed it would pan out. And it did. Our company had 300% growth in revenue and it's because we went all-in on marketing while everyone else stopped. See how the consistency helped us out? We never stopped marketing, and I would certainly say the same to you - don't stop marketing. It's the only way to consistently bring in new clients.

Don't Just Rely on New Techniques

When people go into marketing for their business, they often turn to the newest marketing trend and ignore some of the older techniques that have been around. But it's important to try some of those older marketing trends, especially when everyone is following the same set of rules. When everybody was off of Google Ads because they were shutting people down, I was leveraging their system on Google and making it work by playing their rules.

I continued to use these older methods, and I mastered every one of them. While people were trying to shift to the new, shiny platforms of Tik-Tok and others, we stuck to the basics. If you have a solid grip on your basics, then you do not need to worry about other aspects. I did the same thing on Google and Facebook. Sure enough, the results were far more fascinating than I had imagined.

Back in 2011, we started a company called Funnel Architects. This was before the funnel industry had even taken off. We identified a need for optimization and others started to do the same as us. Needless to say, we've always tried to stay a step ahead. When people were becoming Facebook experts, we were already traffic and funnel optimizers.

The competition was growing, but some of it was bad competition. It become a red ocean with more people entering every day. Everything is trendy now, and as soon as it's trendy it's time to change paths.

For example, complicated funnels are trending. It's what we launched - the one-step funnel. It's an easy way to give a passionate crowd of people the things they love. We started refocusing on our one-step funnel model.

The above may seem slightly off the topic, but the point is simple. Stay a step ahead of the curve and know that you will often need to go back to the basics. Trends and shiny objects will always emerge, but the basics will keep your business running.

Another example is when people focus entirely on new trends. They forget to build the audience, which is the best way to control growth. And you can build audiences with subscriber lists and newsletters, which is what we spend our time focused on.

The idea is fairly simple and does not require you to be a rocket scientist to figure that out. Most of these trends are here for a while before they go obsolete and are lost in the pages of history. Some of these trends remain, and these are the ones we continue to move ahead with as well. We've focused much of our audience building with Email Subscribers.

Marketing is the backbone to any business, and if you own your audience, you will always have people seeing your business.

This goes back to the idea of marketing smarter, not harder. Revenue doesn't become tight if you own your audience. And if Facebook or Google shuts your ad account down one day, you still have an audience to access. Most people don't think this way and rely solely on other people's audiences to generate the revenue for their business.

Sales Momentum

There is a difference between outbound sales and inbound sales. I am what you would describe as an inbound sales guy. Bear with me on this one as I wish to clarify a few things.

A lot of people, whether working with inbound or outbound settings, believe that sales and marketing are poles apart. Frankly, they aren't. You market something, and through that marketing, you generate sales. They are far more interlinked to one another than most would believe.

I pursued inbound marketing because I wanted people to reach out to me. Great marketing does a lot of the selling for us, and it can turn our team into order takers. From emails to videos, there are far too many options for marketing right in front of the customer.

Once you get someone in your whirl, the networks allow you to stay in front of people for as long as you want. This will eventually come to a point where the customer would know you by the mere glimpse of your ad or logo, pushing them to finally click on it and see what you are all about. They want to see if you are offering something that helps them in some way or another.

I know sales and marketing work together, but that it is the marketing that creates the sales and not the other way around. It makes sales a lot easier when marketing is done smart.

Sometimes, You Just Have to Sell

When I went through bankruptcy, I started dabbling in online marketing and trying to figure it all out. I didn't have any money to my name but my friend Mark had the idea to launch a book. He said I had the connections to put it together and gave the model for it. It was the first book I wrote, and I didn't even write it on my own. We interviewed and curated content from seven different experts leveraging my network. I started having conversations with people about putting together a book and if they would like to be involved. I gave the costs and explained what we were doing. We got the entire book paid for and published it pretty quickly. We even launched it up to the number one bestseller.

When we did the pre-launch of the book, I created a relationship with a web guy who gave me some tips on how to generate revenue on a pre-launch. I didn't know what to do, but learned the steps to follow through. I put together a sales page for people to buy in to the pre-launch and ended up selling about $1500 in profit. It was the moment I believed that online marketing was a real, legit thing and that I could do it.

At the time I didn't realize it was marketing. I thought it was just having conversations on the phone. That was tough for me as an introvert, since talking to people on the phone and leveraging networks is not really in my comfort zone.

But it was the moment that I realized I could do work like this from my home, or anywhere else. For about 14 months, my wife and I put everything into storage and traveled around the country. I was building my entire business from a phone and a computer. My momentum started by recognizing the need for money and finding a way to sell.

Marketing and selling go hand in hand. But people don't often like to sell or want to do the hard work of selling. You can create momentum in your sales and generate the revenue you want through joining online groups, finding people you want to do business with, and interacting. If you focus on that interaction, it's going to create momentum for you. Don't go into it with the idea that you want to sell something. Instead, focus on how you want to provide value and the sale will come.

When you gain the momentum of selling, sales come easier to you. It's easy to get into a slump and stop selling because you don't want to deal with it. Maybe you've heard "no" too many times. But you have to get back into the momentum of selling. Marketing makes sales easier and if you don't have any marketing processes in place, you have to be selling anyway. At the end of the day, you need momentum to generate sales. And without sales, you don't have a business. It is all about how you maintain the momentum to keep moving forward. A lot of the people tend to focus on racking up some big sales number, thinking that the rest will happen on their own. While that can happen , it will immediately vanish if you step back and relax a little. You need to maintain that momentum. Stick to your data, routine activities, making the calls, receiving queries, and interacting with potential leads, day in and day out. There is a reason why people often look the other way when they are presented with an opportunity to create a career in sales; it is quite tough. Beyond that tough regime, the numerous calls, and the long hours, you get rewards that are simply unparalleled by any other field in existence. Think about it. The entire world operates through sales. If there are sales, companies will continue to run. If there aren't, every business will come crashing down. To ensure there are sales, you have marketing that backs you up. See how they are interconnected?

If you're struggling to sell, stop looking at the big sale. Instead, focus on smaller ones. Sell someone by setting up a meeting, or having a conversation. That's a win. You have to be willing to weather the storm and find success in the small wins, or you're going to quit.

An addition is to avoid focusing on the sale. If you focus on the sale, you start to become worried about it. When you're worried about it, you'll slowly become desperate to make that sale, and when you're desperate, people will know. You'll lose the confidence you need to successfully make a sale and create momentum.

In the same vein, struggling to make a sale can be focused on how you're trying to give value. Go in with the attitude that you're helping your client. "Hey look man, I see that you're doing this in your business. I think this is something you could do that would be beneficial for you," and tell them how to do it. Just help them. It will generate more leads and sales for you. Taking the focus off you and putting it on them makes a world of difference when it comes to the sales process.

NATE KENNEDY

HIT THE GAS

What is your current marketing process?

_____
_____
_____
_____
_____
_____
_____

How can you improve it?

_____
_____
_____
_____
_____
_____
_____

Go to NateKennedy.com/allgas for a raw, uncut video I recorded for entrepreneurs that want to have Lifestyle Freedom.

""Make your marketing so useful, people will pay you for it."

Jay Baer

Chapter 8

Know the Rules of Engagement

It's important to know the rules before you get involved in a game. And if the rules change, you'd better adapt to them them quickly or lose. This is very true for any business. There are rules that we have to follow to succeed. If we don't, then we lose the business. One of the key lessons I've learned was knowing the rules of engagement when playing the game.

By September of 2010, I had been in the marketing space for a couple of years and had built a pretty solid online presence. So many people, including myself, were enjoying Google traffic, driving them into sales funnels and making a bunch of money. I got to the point where I went out and hired the best of the best in the industry to do the work for me.

At the time I was two days away from getting married and sitting at the rental house we had. A guy I'd hired to run the traffic called me and told me that my account got shut down. They were shutting down all kinds of people in the make-money niche, business-opportunity niche, and different health niches. Google changed the rules of the game and had started banning accounts left, right, and center.

We were buying a decent amount of traffic but weren't like some of the massive companies that got hit by this. I asked what I needed to do to get back online, in which my guy told me that he didn't want to do it since it was a huge hassle. He walked me through what I would have to do including the changing my brand name, landing pages, websites, and how the system was set up. Even then, there was still no guarantee that I would get back online.

I took that advice and looked at the rules to see what else I needed to do. What were the new rules of engagement? What did they want and what didn't they want? There were different types of selling they didn't like, different buzzwords they didn't like, etc.

I recreated the brand and system through their rules of engagement. I started generating leads and then using my email to follow up like I still do today. I was willing to spend and get the leads on the front end, knowing that in the first 30 days I would make money on the back end through the email follow-up campaigns.

I knew most marketers wouldn't do the work to figure out the new rules, and a lot of them just ran off to a new shiny object. I took the time to figure out the rules I had to play by and sat on the Google network almost entirely myself for 18 months. All of my competition was gone and I remember getting an email after 18 months from a guy in the industry. He was shocked that I was still online running ads, and curious how I did it. I did it by not trying to make my money back on day one and waiting for that return by day 30. He wasn't interested in not making money on day one.

That whole experience prepared me later on when something similar almost happened on Facebook. I was with my agency and we were running a bunch of traffic on Facebook. At this time, Facebook was just starting to be a bigger presence in the market space. When they started taking advantage of the network, I started dabbling in Facebook. This was years after Google's regulations and Facebook was a little behind in theirs regulations. They eventually started to do the same thing, banning accounts left and right.

A friend of mine from mastermind even reached out to me and explained that all his accounts were shut down. He asked for my help and we worked together to fix the problem. That phone call resulted in another business opportunity for me. At the time, I was thinking about starting a gym and this guy had owned a bunch of gyms. Our conversation about gyms turned into a suggestion that I should just run Facebook ads for all the gym owners I was meeting with. So that's what I did.

I put together proper website systems, all the pieces, and followed the rules of engagement for Facebook. My experience of doing something similar thing on Google set me up for success when others were struggling.

So many people don't take the time to understand the rules of the game, then try to play. If you take the time to understand the rules, you have an advantage in business. Most people won't want to read the rules and constantly adjust their models to fit.

HIT THE GAS

What are the rules of your game right now?

_____
_____
_____
_____
_____
_____
_____

What rules could you learn more about and take into more consideration?

_____
_____
_____
_____
_____
_____
_____

"The Only Constant in Life Is Change."

Heraclitus

Chapter 9

Mind Your Own Business

Keeping eyes on your own business instead of someone else's is very important, especially if you don't want to lose track of your vision. I like to think of business as an Instagram page. We get to see the perfect image, one that's been slightly (or greatly) retouched and get a glimpse into the perfect world. But we really don't know what's happening behind the scenes. We don't know what it took for people to get to that point in the picture. We have this very beautiful, yet completely unclear image.

For most of us, businesses are just like this. All we ever see is that glossy, beautiful image. We won't know what's happening in the background or what the business did to get to this point. All we ever see is the image they present to us.

One of our clients had an eight-ten million dollar a year business. We did all kinds of massive marketing campaigns for him, and his business looked like it was doing well. He would go to masterminds and had ads running every where. Everyone would compliment on how well he was doing, but behind the scenes, the whole thing was a disaster. However, people don't see that side. They see the ads, marketing, and the superficial face of the business. People didn't have a clue that behind the scenes, everything was different.

You only ever see the front of the business and never what happens behind the curtains. What makes one business work is completely different from another, or even your own. Someone's goals for their business are completely different than your goals for your business.

The downside to only seeing the front of the curtains or a pretty ad is how tempting it looks. You see perfection and think, "I want to do that," or, "I should do something similar." Next thing you know, you've changed your whole business plan and based it on a shallow representation of whatever you're admiring at the time. We have to be careful about comparisons and mind our own business, instead of trying to follow another's footsteps.

Stop looking at what other marketers are doing to run your business. You can't see everything that they're doing, and without the bigger picture, you'll be making decisions based on incomplete data. Focus on your own business, systems, and process.

While you can pick up tips and strategies from other people, mind your business and what your goals are. Always focus on what you want to do with your business and how you want to run it. Define what success means for you, instead of what success means for others. A lot of people trap themselves looking at other companies and thinking that's how their business has to run to be successful. It's easy to assume that everyone successful is perfect, or that all successful businesses are perfect, but it's often not true. So take a step back and remember that what you see in business isn't always what you get.

I learned this the hard way. I was at a mastermind with some other marketers, as well as this one guy I respected highly. I had a lot of respect for his business (the window dressing anyway) and he'd just come out with this new magic funnel. He guaranteed it was going to be a game-changer, or so he said. My partner and I rushed back to change our entire model, which we based our business on, and launched the magic funnel. We only got mediocre results after three months. Another guy at the mastermind also said it didn't work.

I was tricked by the glossy image and window dressing, instead of stopping to look at the whole picture. What he'd created failed because he hadn't tested it out yet. A lot of times people don't want to talk about failure or what didn't work. They only talk about what has worked, or what they hope will work, without giving any backing to it. They present their ideas to look cooler, even if it doesn't work in practice.

I decided to try the magic funnel based on emotions, not data. There was no data to back up that decision and after three months of testing, I had plenty of data to show that it didn't work. I lost time and money but I didn't mind. What we had was working, but I'd changed it because someone else said they had something better.

Minding your own business and staying away from other people's business allows you to focus on your issues and fix things to make them better. When you start looking at other businesses or companies, you try to make decisions based on what you think they're going to do. When you do that, it's just a recipe for disaster.

After those three months, we went back to our original process and built a nice consistent monthly profit. We ended up selling those online assets for over seven figures and I was able to redeem the moment and fix the problem. It was still a headache. However, I did learn a valuable lesson. Focus on your own goals, strengths, abilities, needs, and wants in business. The moment you watch others is the moment you lose all momentum.

If you make decisions based on what other people are doing, you're more likely to end up failing. If we're borrowing ideas, it's because we lack the confidence in our own. You'll learn from the data, and while you may not have 100% success, you will have more success in your goals, than anyone else's.

Also, be careful not to rush the process. It's easy to look over at someone else and see that they're crushing it. You'll want what they have immediately. But there are very very few overnight successes in entrepreneurship. It takes time, energy, focus, and dedication to get there, so keep working towards it, even if it's a slow process.

HIT THE GAS

What is your vision?

_____
_____
_____
_____
_____
_____
_____

How are you catering it to the businesses you're watching?

_____
_____
_____
_____
_____
_____
_____

"The successful warrior is the average man, with laser-like focus."

Bruce Lee

Chapter 10

Keep Your Inner Circle Small

As an introvert, going to large events drains me. Between all of the introductions, handshakes, and networking, by the end of the day I have to be by myself. It's the same even when it's friends and family.

It was hard to put myself in the right rooms. I often ended up in the wrong rooms and put way out of my comfort zone. To progress in business, I needed to meet people and build relationships. I knew I had to get out into a crowd and meet people who had the same thoughts as me. During that process, I quickly learned that not all rooms are created equal.

There are some vultures out there, ready to steal ideas and make a quick buck. I attended one mastermind where I paid $18,000 to attend because I was sold on all the players that were in that room. I believed it would be a perfect fit and I showed up. Those players didn't. When I was in that room, I thought I was in a circle of trust. I presented the business model that I was working on, hoping for some feedback and insight. People gave me recommendations, and one guy even suggested a domain.

After the meeting, I went up to my room to buy the domain. But it was already taken. I decided to see who owns it, since back then you could just look at who bought it. It had been another guy in the room, who'd heard the recommendation and bought the domain name before I could. Later that night, he came up to me and said he liked my idea. He spent the next several minutes trying to get me to use his company and his audience to sell my ideas. I would do the work and they would keep the money.

I was so mad after the first meeting that I never went back, even though I had paid for four meetings a year. I learned a lesson about being in the right rooms and being in the wrong rooms. I found that in some of the rooms, if you were new, you were like the freshman and everyone else was the popular senior. I needed to be more diligent about what rooms I was in because not all rooms were created equal.

Even though that guy tried to sell me my own business, I went off and built it anyway. It did well and I didn't need to use those guys. From that experience, I changed my approach to mastermind meetings and became filled with more focus and purpose. I just wanted to learn, and was really focused on tactics. Over time, I started focusing on the relationships more than the tactics. That is how I found the right rooms and focused on being around the right people, right off the bat. I've met some amazing business people over the years that have all turned to friends.

    While the experience at that mastermind sucked, it also opened my eyes to the real value of being around the right people. It changed my approach to new people and the rooms I put myself in. Keeping the focus on those relationships is how I made businesses profitable. The right relationships, as opposed to the wrong ones, can give you awesome people to work with.

    The values I was looking for back then are a little different now, but I'm always looking for genuine people. People who truly care and are giving value. I'm not looking for people who are busy bragging and pounding their chests with how great they are. I'm not looking for people who are focused entirely on themselves. And there are a lot of people in the entrepreneur world like that. I'm not looking for people who feel the need to prove themselves to others. And I'm not looking for users.

What I look for in the relationships I'm building is going to be different from who you look for. I want to be around the quieter people who have wisdom and advice to share. I'm looking for people who share similar values of being family-oriented, Christian valued, genuine, and focused on giving and providing value. Those are the kinds of people I've always enjoyed working with and being friends with.

I believe I connect with people who share some of the same values that my grandfather did. He was a man I respected growing up and has the values that I still appreciate in people today. He's a good guy who taught me many things about working out, Bible study, and being a genuine person. Everyone loved him because he was humorous, kind, and never flashy. He cared about the people around him and always took care of them. His values are often ones I look for in friends and colleagues now.

I also look for the people who will call me out. If I'm not living up to my potential, I want someone to call me out on it. I want someone to feel comfortable pointing out how I could do better, where I should fix something, or how to stop overthinking things. Great people surround themselves with great people. You are who you hang with. My mom used to always tell me this. Carefully pick the people you associate within your business and life.

Hire & Pay Mentors

You can learn best from others who have done what you are doing. This is why you go to a university, to learn from people in the field you are interested in. It's why people pay for conferences or workshops. Similarly, I recommend that you find and pay mentors to help you progress in your business plans.

Mentors are people who can give you guidance, advice, or inspiration. A good mentor is going after a similar goal to yours, but they're still further ahead. Having a good mentor not only supports your growth, but also increases your connection to others on the same path. Whatever your goals are, find a mentor who is closely connected to that field and can work to improve your skills.

You can benefit from a mentor relationship with the LeapFrog Method. The LeapFrog Method comes from a guy named O'Keefe, who I met back in 2006 at a baseball game. He was in dentistry at the time, but I didn't pay attention to this cool model he had. I met him again six years later at a mastermind and he invited me to come speak at his event. So I set up a presentation about Facebook Ads and he talked about the LeapFrog Method again.

The *LeapFrog* Method is a way to progress faster and learn quicker instead of slogging through difficult steps. It starts with acknowledging where you are at and being honest with yourself. You get the ego out of the way and figure out where to go. When you do this, you might be in a spot you don't like. But that's okay because you're going to learn how to solve it. Find someone already ahead of you, who has done what you've done. Ask them for help and get the knowledge needed to get where they are. Learn from their experiences.

If you pay for someone's knowledge, then you can get to your goals faster, instead of having to go through the same step-by-step process they did. A lot of people don't want to spend that type of money, but not spending it costs you a whole lot more. That's why buying an attorney's time is worth every penny. They will solve so many of your problems and make sure you don't make the same mistakes.
It's the same thing with mentors. They've already been to where you're at so they can see where you're going. They know the roadblocks you're facing and can help you pass through the hurdles.

The only thing that could stop you from doing this, other than finances, is ego. We all have questions and want to know more about where we're going. Our ego can get in the way. It gets in the way of what we're willing to do, which can be a struggle for many. It's hard to ask others for help, especially as entrepreneurs. We feel like we have to do it all ourselves, even though asking for help is a challenge, not a weakness. If you're willing to accept that you don't know everything, then it's easier to go ask the questions you need to figure things out.

Once you have a mentor you're working with, you need to listen to what they're telling you. Don't just say thanks and move on. Actively listen and pay attention to what is being said or done. They might give you an answer that is shockingly simple, but only because you were overthinking the problem in the first place.

Where your money goes is where your attention goes. By hiring a mentor, you are saying that you care about the results. You can take better action because you've spent the money to learn.

When looking for a mentor, start by assessing your goals and what you want from the relationship. Clarify that information and then start looking for someone who meets those requirements. Start within your connections first, and then branch out a little more. Conferences, masterminds, workshops, and training are all good places to meet potential mentors. LinkedIn can also provide information for great mentors.

When you find a potential mentor, you have to approach them and ask for help. This can be daunting, since asking for help doesn't always come naturally to entrepreneurs. Prepare what you want to say and go for it. If you already know your potential mentor well, then your request can be informal and just two friends chatting. But if you're asking someone you're not very familiar with, then you'll want to prepare for the meeting. You'll want to know their background and demonstrate that you're interested in learning from them. Approach it like you would a job interview, with prepared information on your background and goals, as well as an understanding of theirs.

You'll have to clarify some goals for the mentorship and what you hope you'll both get out of it. You can discuss the expectations of the relationship and how often you'll talk. Use your research and preparation time to get a grasp on why this person will make a good mentor for you, then express that to them. What brought you to this person? Explain that and talk it up. Finally, leave them room to decline, which is their right. Whatever their response is, thank them graciously. It's a good idea to have a list of potential candidates you want to reach out to, just in case the first or second ones say no.

Once you've got a yes, it's time to set up the requirements of the meetings. When will you meet? What will be discussed? What's the time commitment? And when will the mentorship end? Discuss all of this carefully and use your goals to stay focused during this planning discussion.

Stop Asking the Wrong Questions

I was at a small, private event with Gary V. who is a prominent entrepreneur. We were having a simple chat and I was really curious about how he kept a work-life balance. Based on the way he talks about work, I knew that balance wasn't really his thing, but it was still curious to me. Balance to me was always being present with my family. I looked at this guy always on a plane somewhere and wonder how he does it. So I asked him. I asked how he keeps his life balanced between work and home. He gave me this long dissertation, but afterward, my buddy looked at me and told me that I had been asking the wrong questions. He said I was asking a guy that had zero work-life balance on how he manages when I should have been asking him questions on how to scale my agency to a hundred million in the next two years.

It was a key takeaway. I had been doing something wrong the entire time I was meeting people. I should have been asking the right questions, and while I was curious about the work-life balance, Gary V wasn't the right person to ask. Instead, I should have been prepared to ask a question related to my business.

When you know you're going to be in a room with a mentor or a coach it's on you to prepare the right questions and gain as much knowledge as you can. When we focus on the wrong questions, we're not learning from the best in the field. If you ask an interesting question, but ultimately not worth much, then you'll get an interesting answer, but ultimately not worth much. It's a wasted opportunity.

I didn't want to waste my opportunity to learn from these people and started preparing questions in advance (especially if I knew who was going to be at these masterminds or in these rooms). I wanted to show them respect by asking the questions relevant to what they do, instead of asking irrelevant but interesting questions.

As a side note, sometimes we want to ask easy questions because we don't want hard answers or answers we don't want to hear. But we can learn best from asking the tough questions, even if the answers are difficult to digest. If you ask the right questions you'll find that those people may want to talk with you more or spend more time around you. High-level people get asked questions all the time and if you are unprepared, then they're not going to remember you or your question, which is a missed opportunity. If you prepare well and ask a good question, they'll remember it and you. So be prepared with your questions before you're in a room with a bunch of other entrepreneurs.

HIT THE GAS

What is your current circle like? What are their values, interests, intentions?

_____
_____
_____
_____
_____
_____
_____

What values, interests, and intentions do you want to be more surrounded by?

_____
_____
_____
_____
_____
_____
_____

"You are the average of the five people you spend the most time with."

Jim Rohn

Chapter 11

The Non-Negotiables

I want to end this book on the things that are semi-permanent in life: your values. I'm calling them semi-permanent because they do change over time, but are often the hard and fast rule you live by at any point in time. Your values, both personal and business-focused, are the framework for everything you do. So you must be aware of what your non-negotiables are. Where do you draw the line?

As a business owner you're going to be tested every day. Within those tests are failures that present themselves as opportunities. People will pull you in all different directions where you ultimately end up working 18-hour days. It can happen very quickly. If you don't set your non-negotiable ahead of time, you'll quickly find yourself swept away by everything else.

The non-negotiable are the things you value. They can be the goals for your business, your morals in practice, values, and so on. Without these non-negotiable in place, you end up focusing on just making money in a business that is no longer aligned with your values or business morals. Your non-negotiable helps guide your decisions and saves you massive amounts of time in the long run. Every decision you make can be looked at against your non-negotiable. You can determine if a decision does or doesn't fit within the core values you've set.

One of my main non-negotiable is family first. I already talked about how important work-life balance is for me, and now I can't emphasize enough how this value is important to me too. At home, I have my wife, and two children, a boy, and a girl. I've seen a lot of businessmen turn into terrible fathers by always working or traveling. If they are not there for their kids, how do they grow a good relationship with them? What about all the missed life events because of work? I don't want to ever have to tell my kids that I can't be home because I have to work. And I don't want to ever miss a birthday or special event because I'm doing something work-related. I want to be there for my children and wife every day. The only way I can do this is by setting my boundaries and making sure that they're non-negotiable.

I chose this non-negotiable early on and knew this one from growing up. It was instilled in me by my parents and my grandparents. I knew that I always wanted to be there when I had kids. As a kid, my parents were always present for sporting games and extracurricular events. I want to be there for my kids and maintain a good work-life balance.

I remember my dad always working so hard. He would come home during the week and just zone out in front of the TV. I remember him being burnt out that I knew I didn't want that in my own life. I wasn't willing to grind out 18 hours a day and not be engaged with my kids. I wanted to be fully present and aware of each moment with them. So I spend time with them. We go on vacations as a family and do activities together. We snowboard, surf, hang at lakes and go camping. We do things together as a family because it is so important to our ever-developing relationship. My family and family time is non-negotiable for me.

Another non-negotiable is consistently working out. The more I exercise my body, the better my brain gets. To me, a good training or exercise gets the blood flowing. I didn't learn this one right out of the gate. Instead, I learned this one later. I used to train for football in the summer and fall. When sports ended for me after graduating, I knew I wasn't going to play in college. So I decided to stop working out altogether. I didn't work out for about 12 years.

When my son was born I decided to hire a coach, Drew Canole, the guy who owns FitLife TV and Organifi. I wanted to get healthier, especially since a friend of mine had passed away at the same age. Drew came to my house, went through my pantry, and gave me a meal plan. I went all in. I wanted to get in shape. I did the 90-day transformation and was so focused on working on it that I lost 40lbs. I went from 28% body fat to 6.8% body fat. But what stood out the most was that my business tripled. I looked at the data and realized that fitness and being healthy had to be non-negotiable. I needed to exercise my body and my brain.

To this day, I've found that missing a workout is reflected in my attitude, in a non-positive way. It's another reason why fitness is non-negotiable. I'm in a better mindset and state of being.

We have to put non-negotiable into place, otherwise, we'll be working ourselves to death. It's easy to fall into the grind of working a 24/7, 365 lifestyle, but one of my non-negotiable is not doing that. Been there, done that, and when you learn to do less, you learn that you don't need to hustle that much. There's no badge of honor for hustling 24/7.

I believe that defining your personal non-negotiable will allow you to make better business decisions. because

ALL GAS, NO BRAKES

Opportunities will always offer themselves, but you have to be willing to say no to the wrong ones. It's very easy to say yes, and the more you say yes, the more time you are dedicating to it. The non-negotiables give you the framework for control over those decisions.

Your non-negotiable can change over time, or you may even break them to reach short-term goals. They're not static but they should be defined. Where you are today is not where you'll be in ten years. Understand that your non-negotiable will change and adapt as much as life. You still take the time to define them and use them as the framework for your life.

HIT THE GAS

Establish your non-negotiables.

ALL GAS, NO BRAKES

"You get what you tolerate."

Henry Cloud

NATE KENNEDY

Conclusion

Whether you are an expert in sales, marketing, or services, there is much to learn for everyone. Learning has never stopped; and it never will. That is how the world works, and that is how I tend to go with my personal and professional life as well.

Between joyfully playing in pools of profits to when the entire world came to a screeching halt, I've been in this game for a while now. During those times, entrepreneurs, business professionals, and service providers were all worrying about how to save their assets and protect their capital, while some, like a friend of mine, were contemplating suicide. Why? I too was in the same boat but not once did I give up on what I wanted to do. When the world crashed, I stood up to the challenge. Yes, I was suffering too, in fact, I had to resort to bankruptcy, something that I had never envisioned in my life, (or even in my wildest dreams). However, I knew it was something beyond my control, and that I had to learn from it. There's no point in dwelling about the things you could've done differently. I always knew where I had to go, what I had to do, just to get back on track.

Through my journey, I met some incredible people, one of them being Mark, who guided me, mentored me, and showed me how I could regain my stride and get back at the very top of the game. Needless to say, I was making millions once again!

I have often seen young entrepreneurs struggling with the simplest of things. They go searching the internet trying to learn from the so-called gurus, false prophets, and self-proclaimed success stories, but fail to see the answers right in front of them. All they need to do is to review their numbers, and the rest will fall into place. It is saddening to see that a lot of these young men and women are misled, especially by people see their ideas and concepts as threatening. They would storm these young brains with negativity and try to knock them over. Those who cave, give up on their visions. However, those who continue to persevere, as I did, often find out that the people who once criticized their ideas are the same ones adopting it.

People are easily manipulated. And while most of that has to do with a weak emotional state, it isn't something to be ashamed of either. You can always improve on the control over your emotions, and how you would respond to given situations. With that said, you must learn how to control your emotions and keep them at bay when you are catering to serious matters, especially about your business ventures. There is only room for one. You can let emotions dictate you or use them to make effective decisions.

Never go on to compare yourself with others. The fact is that there is never a true competition because everyone is unique. Everyone has their core values, which means that a successful model for me might not work for you. I may be following a set of core values that aren't the same as yours.

Your team is your biggest asset. Treat them with respect and care. It is these men and women who pour in all the efforts to ensure that your business goes on to achieve great success. Instead of undermining or ignoring them, try to empower them. Make great leaders out of everyone, and allow them to take the lead to prove their worth. If you reward them with promotions, appreciation, and bonuses, you are sure to keep their motivations and spirits high. The happier the worker, the better your business operates.

Those who often wonder if they have enough money to market their products and services or not, know that marketing is the backbone of any business. Even if you do not have any budget for marketing, do things the old-fashioned way and reach out to your leads and potential customers. Instead of sharing your sales pitch right away, take time out to interact with people and get to know them. This will provide you with value and help too. If you do that, you can sell whatever offer you want, as long as it is relevant. This is why many successful businesses invest hundreds of thousands of dollars in marketing, just to ensure that they can attract the right kind of leads and maximize their conversion rates. Marketing equals sales, and there is no other way to put this.

It is always tempting to take a peek into someone else's business model, financial standings, and so on. It is that 'juicy' gossip that you often get to see on the television, but let me be the first one to tell you; just mind your own business. There is absolutely nothing that you can gain out of poking into other's business because it takes time, energy, and resources to do so. If you are smart, you would rather use those resources to do something more productive.

Do not be drawn in by the shiny object syndrome. Just because Tik-Tok might be in trend these days does not mean that you should jump ships and invest a significantly large amount of money into it. These trends are usually short-lived and flocked by other competitors, meaning you will not have an edge over your competition.. There are only two ways you can go about things. You can either stay ahead of the curve by a step or two, or you can retrace your steps and stick to the basics. Ideally, you should be able to do both because there will come a time where you will need to step back just to see the complete picture and sticking to the basics. You'll need plenty of time to figure out your next big move.

Next, it comes down to the kind of people you choose to spend your time with. If you wish to be truly successful, you have to step out of your comfort zone, introduce yourself, and create relationships. It is through these relationships that you will get to maximize your earning potential and find leads that will help you move ahead. Of course, you will always have the quality leads leads you generated through marketing campaigns..

Finally – Mentors! You want them, you need them, and you cannot expect to grow your business, without them. Mentors are the people who were once where you are today. They have been in the same situation and gone on to achieve an extremely successful status in life. You can find many great mentors, but not all of them are right for you. Depending on the field you choose to work in, hiring a mentor is based on experience, knowledge, and success. These are the kind of people who will teach you, guide you, and help you become a better entrepreneur, business professional, and individual. Through their guidance, you will go on to achieve the next level in your life. Once you reach that level, find another mentor that is a level higher, and learn from that person, and so on.

Being an entrepreneur means that you have to learn for the rest of your life.Every profit you make, and every loss that comes your way will be a learning opportunity for you. Learn what needs to be learned, and apply the knowledge in your life.

ALL GAS, NO BRAKES

I have shared some of the stories that I would normally keep to myself. and I have done so only to hope that I go help new entrepreneurs find their stride and learn from my experience. They can apply the knowledge I have shared and feel ensured that they do not go through the long, winding, guessing road. Now you know what you need, and you know how much it can do for you. It is up to you to decide when you want to start acting on it. I wish you nothing but the best, and hope that this book goes on to help you for ages. Stay safe!

When in doubt, never let your foot off the gas.

Made in the USA
Middletown, DE
30 June 2022